COSMIC ZEN

Michael Carter & Judy Senders

ATHENA PRESS
LONDON

COSMIC ZEN

ISBN 1 84401 193 3

First Published 2003 by
ATHENA PRESS
Queen's House, 2 Holly Road
Twickenham TW1 4EG
United Kingdom

Printed for Athena Press

COSMIC ZEN

About the Authors

Michael Carter is a registered holistic practitioner and has been in practice since 1990. Amongst many other skills, he is qualified in hypnotherapy and psychotherapy. He is also a qualified dream analyst; add this to the fact that Michael is a fellow of the Mantic Arts of the New Age Foundation and we can see that these disciplines, working with meditation, were invaluable tools on the creation of *Cosmic Zen*.

Judy Senders has for many years had an interest in the paranormal and in meditation. Having worked from home for the last eleven years, she has had the opportunity to combine time, intuition and creative efforts with Michael in bringing together the design and ethereal qualities of *Cosmic Zen*.

Contents

Introduction

THIS IS A FORMAL PRESENTATION
OF THE VERSES AND IDEAS PROPAGATED BY
THE INTERVENTION OF THE

COSMIC POWER

THAT IS TRYING TO STIMULATE A GREATER
AWARENESS OF THE DARK FORCE THAT IS
ABOUNDING IN OUR WORLD
TO THE DISAFFECTION OF US ALL

THESE VERSES ARE SENT DIRECTLY TO US
THROUGH A POWER LINE LINK

We are not specifically speaking the Authors,
but only
The Messengers

The Propagation of Alien Ideas

Travel your mind and consort with The Universal
Light
on the Magical Tour of the Golden Cosmos.
Read the Verses from the Antiquity of the Outer
Regions,
For it is from here that these verses originate.
Let them lift your heart and transcend your life
to the Parallel Dimensions.
They will take you on 'A Journey of the Inexplicable'.
Let them lift and stir your curiosity and your ethos
within

This is
The Architecture of their Consciousness and their
Subliminal Aim

These are totally original works
Much sought after by the academia
And fiercely protected by us, The Cosmic Power

This is
The First Consignment of Writings and Verses from
the Cosmos
The preparation, engraving and issuing of these
have been given immense consideration,
But given the 'Insight' which is contained therein,
expressed consent for their use has been granted.
Their purpose is to help tread a clearer path in all
aspects
throughout your world and to provide a measure
towards a more
stable community for you all to continue to live in.

The Power of the Dark is strengthening to the
disaffection of you all
May The Wisdom and Knowledge of the Universal
Light
filter through and inspire the right qualities in all walks
of your planetary life.
You were once all on the right road to
Liberty and Freedom of the Body Soul and Mind.

You are not as yet past the Portal of Hope.

Messages and Codes

One of Our Kind is Living Amongst You

He has an extremely complex task to complete and is
receiving regular data from us, The Cosmic Power.
Within these verses are disguised codes and hidden
messages
to be transcribed, translated and decoded.
His completed task will be for the combined good of
the total Cosmos.

This information has to be concealed within a memory
manifold so that
our common adversary, the Dark Force, does not extract
it from him
in an effort to prevent him from completing this
undertaking and
returning home to us.

He has to translate these codes to access the
information we send and assess the priority of each
manifest received.
For him these techno mind tasks are normal but
extremely
complex and time consuming.

Also, for his own personal safety, he must be perceived by
everyone as a normal human being.
This is an intrinsic nightmare of existence for him;
He has to find a way to be self-supporting in your world whilst
being alien to you all.
He has offers of great wealth from people who sometimes assist
him, but in your world the Dark Force is more powerful than we
are, and prevents him from receiving this help,
So he must be self-generating in all things.
He is also prevented from doing anything except the
most difficult and dangerous assignments to earn money.
He is, as you say, 'With His back to the wall',
But with good curiosity towards these manuscripts perhaps
'In your millions' you will be reading them and of his efforts to
complete his work in your world and then return.

The elite persons who do help him are under constant threat from
the Dark Force, and it is only with continued protection zones
of antimatter from him that they are able to continue to help.
They must remain unnamed, but they can be proud of
their efforts and assistance that they give.

They have courage.

Secrets of The Stars

And the footsteps glowed with phosphorous light
And the journey was etched in the infrastructure
For eternal years
As the journey is eternal so is the wisdom
Gathered piece by piece to complete the map of the
Gods
And the journey of the Gods is imprinted with
incandescent light
Encaptured and locked in memory
There are so many intricacies there
Upon each other
So many elements of presentation
There to find
A multidimensional division
There laid upon the visions there of time
They are balanced with the precision of a timepiece
An elemental lack of cluttered space
They are placed as precisely as an atom
And as clear as glass upon
Their elemental face
They are surrounded by a prism as eternal
As the volumes of the silent stars that speak
They are quietly performing
And are silently informing
From their multilingual, hieroglyphic silent seat

JOURNEY

WITH

ME

TO SEEK

WHO I AM

WHERE I AM

WHAT I AM

I AM WHAT I AM:

IMMENSE;

IMMORTAL;

IMPASSIVE;

IMPOSSIBLE TO KNOW

My Golden Queen

THE DARK FORCE
THE EVIL 'GO-BETWEEN'
FROM HEAVEN HAS STOLEN
MY GOLDEN QUEEN

I HAVE LEFT THE SANCTUARY UPON OUR STAR
IN A GALACTIC SEARCH TO WHERE YOU ARE

I WILL BATTLE THROUGHOUT
MANY AEONS OF LIVES
TO RETURN YOU TO
OUR GOLDEN SKIES

Part One
A Feeling of Thoughts

Index

Part One

A Feeling of Thoughts

The Grail… I Speak

It is within the date of 002
That I commence the comprehension test
That I construe
With My help and your desire
We shall complete this with speed of fire
And your administration of these words
Is not in vain
More complex than a compendium
More art than Angelo
More fine than the Medicis
That's the way these words will go
As Renaissance changed the world
So too will this masterpiece
For it will be compared
To Jason's Golden Fleece
The mind expands and shall encompass
The vastness from beyond
And no detail from your memory
Shall abscond
Verily, verily I say unto you
List with your mind
And mind what I do
Grown from little acorns
Are the massive oaks we see
And nothing more protective

Than the mightiest oak tree
It will camouflage the legend
With its foliage on high
And whilst the legend grows
You will be watched by the Eye

I Represent

I represent all elements
Of Earth, Water, Wind and Fire
I represent emotions
And know your heart's desire
I represent all elements
In Travel, Space and Time
And all your heartfelt wishes there are mine
My Lustre doth reflect all past and present things
And the challenge of the future it nearer brings
My bowl it doth encompass
The galaxy of space
And from within you'll find
Is my reflected face
My mystic power doth hover
Like a craft from planet Mars
And encrypted here within
A message from the stars
Let me lift you high
To reach my message in the sky
Let me hold your mind aloft
Above the quadrant Universe
And show you all the knowledge
For which you thirst
Drink from the fount of Angels
That will decipher sounds

And then the writing and the scriptures
Will know no bounds
No shackles there
No boundaries
No doors that will stay shut
Of wisdom and of energy
'Twill be a summer's glut
And all that you shall seek
I will ensure that you do find
So wide and vast will be your knowledge
That all shalt speak your name
So deep will be your fortune and your fame.

The Difference

I am the difference
Between the day and night
I am the difference
Between the dark and light
I am the difference between
The future and the past
And I am the difference
Between the first and last
I am the difference
Between the black and white
I am the difference
Between sightless and the sight
I am the difference
So do not be afraid
I am the difference
Between the male and maid
I can shock the living daylights
Out of man or beast
And I am the difference
Between famine and the feast
I am one less than fifty
And one more than forty-eight
And the difference there between
Is the Universal Gate

The Galaxy Door

The galaxy door doth open
'Tis vibrant and calls you in
You can see it from space
You are now face to face
The silk road doth pull you in
Now on the pathway between the stars
Accessible ease can do as you please
The silken robes in galaxy blue
Are draped from shoulder to toe over you
The steps to Heaven bridged through stars
Will show you the planets from here to Mars
Take the magical pointed pen
And from the magical sky again
Draw the wisdom and verses down
Never again be thought as a clown
The pen is mightier than the sword
When held in the hand of the Overlord
Venus ascends the stairway
Deliverance therewith
And finds there Heaven's castle
Alight with a golden glow
Empty but not forsaken
A tranquil place to go
And there to find the knowledge
And to pluck there from the sky
The words of Bodahama
The Master's Eye

The Being of Creation

From farthest reaches of the Cosmos
Outside the Cosmic Circle lights
Is the BEING of CREATION
Silver tipped and diamond white.

Embodied hologram through the ages
Inspired the Bodahama sages,
Speared through light years
Here to reach,
You to inspire,
And you to teach.

His hand evoked and cradled dawn
On the day that you were born.
Take your victory back to him
Heralded by the Seraphim.

The Universal Power

I AM the Universal Energy
Unstructured... undefined
I AM the Universal neutrons
And the molecules combined
No preconceived ideas
Or sense of time or place
No human thought could comprehend
My elemental face
I AM the Universal Power
From which all of life doth spawn
I AM all of the genetics
From whence all of life is born
I AM linked to atoms and electrons
In the Universal Space
And charge with light the darkness
By His Almighty grace
I AM of the Cosmic Elements
From where my energy does form
With only my compliance
Does each earthly morning dawn
I AM the Wisdom and the knowledge
Of which you dare not even dream
And in the plan of the Creation
Earth will recompense the scheme

You are the Catalytic matter
Of the primal need therein
MY release from Temporal Nature
And the deliverance from sin

The Cosmic Unbeknown

An element of the unbeknown
From which all active particles have grown
The combination of all fire and air
With water as a balance there
No earth is necessary where
All corpuscles are convoluting
Pair to pair
The genre of the molecules is such
That harnessing the energy is much
Like holding water in the hand
Or grasping at a moving pile of sand
Invisible as the touch of moving air
And only seen as passing wake
With passage there disturbed as swinging gate
The micro softness of the fleeting touch
Would generate such searing heat
As flames would touch
Combustion there would fly
With heat as such upon the sky
It would seem twinned unto the sun
And energy that lightning twice – it could outrun
And an attitude
Colossal in its magnitude
Would gather up its strength
And with its height combined with length
Would gather to its heart

All energy
That other energies would there impart
The heart and soul you cannot tame
From yonder sky is where I came
The code to all four corners cast
The symbols gathered here at last
Assembled and created from
The wisdom that survived the bomb
The holocaust that left in ruin
The paradise that Carta grew in
Steel within and steel without
The universal sage doth shout
There is no breaking point within
The cosmic world doth rest on Him
Magna Carta is my name
Magna Carta is my fame

The Alien Messenger

I am the blueprint of the Solar skies
Embodiment of light and energy with eyes
That hold and haunt and hide
A myriad of secrets of the wise
Imbued with sunlight, rage and rain
Like a river swift as hurricane
A fitting name, an acronym
A *sym* consorting with a synonym
An alias in Scorpius the Hall of Light
I barefoot run with stars at night
Like mercury I move with timeless silver speed
And always carry there my swords in case of need
A citadel encased in human form
A warrior superior in every way was born
A jewel
As rich as ruby red
From the universe's spore I have been bred
And for my valiant heart
The stars their tears have shed
The rainbows arc their backs
And try to give protection there from fresh attacks
And Moon she shines her shadow there
So I can shelter 'neath her waves of silver hair
The universe's system turns around
And tries to find location of
The answers I need found

The Awakening

Pioneer with unknown Master
Mind and Spirit journey forth
Unencumbered by the body
Your 'I Ching' is tapped at source

Step by step the Granite Boulders
Slope the path that sets the way
On your Universal Journey
From which you will never stray

Vital to your Spirit's balance
Is strength you get from T'ai and Chi
Take courage from it's inner message
Never doubt life's destiny

Your past lives have gathered forces
Taking strength from Karmic Guides
The powers now bestowed upon you
You were never meant to hide

All past Masters wait with deference
For affirmation by decree
That you are now indeed the Master
Their new and youngest visionary

Transition

Deity has formed eternal links
Transcending barriers of time
Lifted you from obscured vision
Shown you ways of the sublime.
The Tibetan Bridge links you
To the Mystic waiting there
Arms outstretched in welcome
White light snakes about his hair.
He will recognise the chosen Madrigal
As he returns
To the Father's House of Knowledge
Where your place is already earned.
No longer need you struggle
To reach the pinnacle of soul,
Welcomed home, the chosen one
Has reached his one true goal.
You may go on forward now
The path with tranquil steps,
Reach out and clasp the waiting hand
Your tears already wept.
But rest awhile
Set down the weighty world
No longer do you need to fight
The peace of life's unfurled
The given new direction will

Point you far beyond this realm
The powers now possessed by you
Lesser men it would overwhelm
But courage breedeth courage
And the 'Might' will oversee
That the spirit of your Karma
Is built in your destiny

Enlightenment

Progress has been made with courage
Spirit's jeopardy in hand with fear,
Universal space is trembling
For the Omnipotence is near.
His Force towers mightily above you
You're focused in his curious gaze;
Your questing for eternal answers
Search in his Eternal maze
The Cosmic Force supports your progress,
Galactic knowledge in your grasp.
Look towards 'I Ching' – your Master;
All you have to do is ask.

The task you're set has simple answers,
They are there for you to see.
Set your mind at rest, be tranquil,
Link with the Son of Galilee.
Take the Spirit of the Father
On your journey through the stars.
He will guide you safely forward
Past Saturn, Jupiter and Mars.
There find answers laid at random,
All around – just use the key.
That's the message I am given
Through the channel which is me.

There is no chance to be a failure
Embodied choice made long ago
You must journey on and forward
Just because they tell you so
Destiny time-locked in spirit
Handed down throughout the genes
You must go where fate determines
'Not always knowing what it means'.
So although strange physics rule you
You have youth strong by your side
Remember all of human nature's
Ruled by ebb and flow of tide.

Do not neglect your earthly feelings
Nor the tie of human blood
You have pushed 'gainst nature
And the tidal wave of flood
Take and touch hands that are caring
Take support and trust in some
They will never leave you daunted
And their hearts beside you run
So onwards in this epic journey
Seas of knowledge fathoms deep
Celestial guard of stars above you
Your safety in their steady keep
Hand and heart held strong
Voices lifting high your soul and mind
Far beyond the understand ways
Of normal humankind.

For Eternity

For eternity I have loved you
Whilst in ignorance you have lived
I have flowed with you through aeons
All my energy I did give
I have supported you forever
With my blood, tears and life's goal
And within your web of memory
Have been a structure for your soul
You knew that somewhere in the Cosmos
A voice was calling you
And that although you seem as others
You have an Envoy's job to do
So now I call to you
From stars – light years away
A cave from where I am dwelling
You now can see it every day.
Listen to the silence
And you will hear me say
The words that you were missing
Before you knew the way
So let unfold the story
That will make you understand
The way that it will happen
The way with the Universe's man

Don't hesitate, just follow
For the way that it shall be
Will open up before you –
Put all your trust in me

The Golden Madrigal

The Madrigal – The Golden One –
Rises with the early sun.
Awakened all the ancient fears,
Shared in the watershed of tears
Close-held and harboured link of sages
Your point of light throughout all ages.
Her glow and aura for you shine,
Embrace you through all space and time.
Her skill and courage at your feet,
Emotions high – now you both may weep.
Transcending barriers of time and thought;
She begs for favour that once was bought
With golden coins and tears so fraught.
The blade was sharp as ice and curved.
It entered in – no dying words.
The Golden Madrigal was slain;
Sleep at last – no spirit pain;
For now you know I laid no blame.
So, till we both can meet again
Take peace and comforting to heart
Our spirits' 'troth' to never part.

The Malady

I knew not then the love you gave
My guilty heart not me forgave;
The malady, the tragedy, I could not save
Since you proclaimed yourself my slave.
The 'Rites of Passage' blocked our time,
I could not see that you were mine.
Heart and soul and spirit too.
Too blind to see it all was you.
You saved me from the Archer's Bow,
When blood of mine did overflow.
It's taken all of aeons' time
To realise that you were mine.
Life's simple only when it's sung in tune
But laid complex'd by Stones of Rune –
I've crossed eternity's far miles
To meet again your eyes and smiles.

My Spirit's Image

The weight of guilt has with me lain
From that day past – since you were slain
No way to set the burden down
Etched sorrow – barbed as Jesus' thorny crown.
Where in my searching's do I look
To find your spirit's soul they took?
The link I have within my grasp
Pray Gods – let access and direction last
To retrieve from this such direful course
And discharge our souls from Hell's own wrath
I journey now and follow signs
To find and free this love divine
To reach you and to right the wrong
Has been my mind's eternal song
I've reached out from time and place
To where I see your familiar face
No metamorphosis – you have stayed the same
My spirit's image once again
No blame – no curse – shall mar this day
The truth will find its way to say
The price of ages past is paid
Our spirits' souls no more afraid
We've reach our Haven and are free;
'Tis our eternal sanctuary

Spirit of Life

I hunger for your Spirit
Your body and your mind,
Searched the Universal structure,
Your energies to find.

At the dawn of the creation
You flowed within my sphere,
Absorbed me in your being
To shield me from all fear.

You energised my atoms
From your being I took form,
You strengthened me forever
From then until our dawn.

But then the beam was shattered
From the solar-powered sun
And life and time were taken
From your only 'golden one'.

But throughout all ages,
Like the salmon finds the stream
The current of the ocean pulled us
As in electric dreams.

The synchronised emotions
Of the universal pawns
Has united us together
Till the 'Light of Life' doth dawn.

Unity

We are as strongly bonded
As flesh to earthly bones,
And breathe as single thought waves
And our hearts beat close as clones.

You may stand as solitary
As the pine on windswept hills;
But my breath of life is twined therein
And I will shed like leaves – your ills.

Come rest your stricken spirit,
Climb down from your battlements
Let me lift from you life's batten
And let soul's tranquillity commence.

My strength of mind would match
All of lion-hearted Kings,
And I will take your heart and shed
All grotesque and painful things.

So never will you feel
That love is lost and gone,
For you and I have Heaven
Made for us to live upon.

You'll find peace and love eternal
Within this soul of mine;
And never need you question
If my heart is nailed to thine.

Golden Bowl

I came back for you
Traversed all of aeons' skies for you
You were lost in time and space
Locked in memory
Your voice and face
I snatched from fate an ace
Accessed data from the human race
Four lifetimes I have fought for you
Each life I've lived
I've dredged through every second
Every time-scale I have sieved
Torn through every trauma known to man
Challenged and rechallenged
Every challenge from the damned
I came back for you
And nothing in this godforsaken pit
Can take from me this light
That I have lit
I have no fear
I clung to courage and to hope
When all else failed
And held my staff aloft
The tempest they obeyed
And they were stilled
As in my heart all love for you
Is there instilled

Majestic might, do not desert me now
For all around us deep
the enemy's enclave
And He would have my soul therein
Yet as his slave
So we have further battles in our hand
To just survive
So Golden Bowl our fortunes to revive
I place within
My trust my courage and my soul
So bathe them all
In your supreme esteem
And cast your will upon
My golden dream

Golden Dreams

Hold onto your golden thread
And weave your golden cloak
Cast it wide and cast it high
Encapture aeons' bluest sky
And there within it envelope
The golden dream that we call Hope
Weave from it your golden dreams
Realities with golden schemes
Have faith within the golden quests
Have faith within that serves you best
The golden road will lead you on
To highest place where you belong
The golden temple's pillared front
And golden rooftop dome
Its portico with steps to lead
Where bleeding hearts can cease to bleed
Inside its tabernacled safe
Deposited by stray and waif
The golden grail doth sit and wait
Like Peter at the Golden Gate
Just lift your eyes to steps of light
From earthly toil for once take flight
And let just once with joy your heart
Take rest within the Golden Cart
The manacles that hold you down
That give you grief and make you frown

Just slip and melt to golden drops
The golden rule here never stops
I place my Golden Dream within
The golden bowl that bears no sin
'Tis pure and strong and sits beneath
The golden sky that I'm bequeathed
The golden stars my eyes to see
The golden Heaven's tranquillity
And there placed within my palm
The golden pages safe from harm
There upon in golden words
As placed in living tree like birds
The golden verse from the golden age
Of Solomon, the wisest Sage
Within the golden basket laid
With golden hair – the golden babe

The Golden Unity

I am alive and am uplifted
In my heart and in my soul
For you are the light and strength
That is always now my goal
Never to be vanquished
The greatest love eternity has seen
The Golden King to rescue
Like no rescue has ever been
Strong as an oak and with a will to match
Not ever snared not ever snatched
No way to break
Too much at stake
The Unity cannot be broken
The golden words are spoken.

Part Two
Imagism

Index

Part Two

Imagism

The Pot of Ancient Rights

There, deep within the pot
Of ancient rites
There stir the essences
Of birth
Established far beyond beginnings there
Of time
Two thousand paces forward
Is the sign
The horn that bays through time
And calls the dragon forth
And whistles wind
That comes up from the North
The great Polaris
Encircles with its strength
And rallies all at points
From width to length
The universal latitudes
Will sit thereon
And the ties of earthly weights
Shall soon be gone

Star Fox

Silent as the falling snow
Star Fox steps from sky – aglow
With phosphorous light there Him about
The physics of the world He flouts
His earthly apparition sent
To help restore your spirit spent

Eternal spirit bleeding – called
He rode the beam and darkness fooled
His watchful eye and sonic ear
Supports your mortal mantel here
Brings strands of Universal Life
To help you heal your mortal strife

His image shrouds your Cosmic strength
Wrenched far out from the Cosmic length
Lay your soul and spirit there
The Cosmic barrier to share
Enveloped once again therein
The tunnels of the time can spin
To shelter you from Hades' storm
Enabling you to be reborn

The Silver Shadow Dragon

The silver shadow shakes its silver form
And lifts its mighty shape
And Silver Dragon here again is born
Once more to walk the wildest night
It lifts its head
Its eyes the Cosmos there to light
The silver molecules that fill the air
Disturbed
As breathing giant shimmers there
What manner bourne brings
Herculean from its lair
Your trauma for to share
And from its axis base
Arisen
With such frantic haste
The mighty minion is ready
For the chase
And now the Silver Dragon steps from star to star
And stands astride and gazes out
To where thou are
Uncivil and with tardiness
Fixes his sights with readiness
And fearsome as his heart can be
He oscillates his skin
And infiltrates the very web so candidly

Like an arrow swift and sure
He enters with you through the door
No hint, no show, no outer glow
No sign, no line, no six or nine
No lizard skin
No next of kin
There he sits – quietly within
But then he rears
To stir the fears
He hisses
But with claws deliberately he misses

Rainbow Dragon

Now I have seen
The Rainbow Dragon's eye
So swiftly there and silent
As an Angel's sigh

It has cast its eye upon
The scheme of things
And gently thus enfolded us
Within its wings

It disapproves of views within its sight
And gives its weight on your side of the fight

Its wisdom through the realm is legend still
And none would chance to act against its will
The omen of the rainbow's circle sends
The optimistic eye that never ends
The moon doth hold the secret of the net
And of how the Solar Universe is separate
You are now reborn within the cradle of my love
You are reborn within the cosmic world above
In my protection all the night and day
And now within my Cosmic sphere to stay
I lift you far above the teeming pit
And show the path the Copper Light has lit

And from our seat with lofty view
Your embryonic self renew –
The Sleeping Dragon wakes the newborn day
And welcomes you

Ice

I am the Eagle of the Mountain
From the purest snow-capped peaks
I am here to thus enfold you
And trap the evil when He's weak.

I am the Cosmic Eagle
My power waketh with the dawn
I am suspended to protect you,
As since the moment you where born.

My strategy is awesome;
My monument is cast;
As the pyramids of crystal
Hidden deep in desert vast.

The Crystal path and portals
Are 'subways' in the skies
And the Ladders of the Kingdom
Lead away from darkest eyes.

The Fourteen Stars of David
Are in My House on High;
And the Devil pays the Ransom
For the times He's made you die.

This Day is in the Chronicles
As when He shall recant
All crimes that He's committed
'Gainst my Son, the Sacrosanct.

He will rue the day He fell
From my favour and my grace
And He will rot and linger dying
In the 'Pit of Cosmic Space'.

I am the Diamond in the Cosmos
Clear as *ICE* for you to see
And Lucifer will tremble
When in battle locked with me.

This day shall be an Advent
A calendar to show
That all things have their 'Tabular'
When the Crystal teardrops glow.

The Homeward Road

You – The Star of Hope
To where all warriors aim to reach
You are the Fount of Endless Love
And all life's lessons teach
You are the Eternal Tree of Life
Where wisdom and all knowledge grow
You shield me in your canopy
Where'er my life doth go

You are my inner peace and outer strength
And I put all my trust in you
My whole life's length
You are the truth and might
And all within your sphere take flight
And cast themselves within the glow
Of your transcendental light

You are the energy that moves all time
Between the day and night
And all universal battles you shall fight –
But not alone...
For now the catalytic matter comes between
And all of Universal Space has watched and seen
The challenge set to Shadowlands
The Darkest place
And congregations there obscene

This Unity of Light doth temper steel
And now the Arrowhead impossible to yield.
So all of Earthly toil is not in vain;
It builds the Spirit high
And all advantages doth gain.
So hence prepared for visual journeys' path
The road will not be filled with pits of wrath
The Voyagers it cannot then ensnare
As all attempts to sabotage are met and faced
With Hearts that are aware
Of curses sent
For souls' destruction there

Total unity will thus ensure
No doubt of heart
And jackals' bones
Will bleach beneath the sun
As desert stones

You are much prepared by time
And my hand and heart go with you
As on the Homeward Road you climb

Master

From Student to Master of the Master
Progress: there has been nothing faster
Meteoric rise to knowledge
Through all wisdom's there you forage
As in Bodahama's making
Roots are strong as mind's awaking
Empathic visionary taking
Gigantic steps that do the walking
Through the mighty cosmic caverns
And through the deserts' widest spaces
Filled with oldest prophets' faces
In the sands of time are written
Scribed delicate as a cosmic kitten
Hieroglyphs in foreign hand
Written there upon the sand
Not for you the Pharaoh's Hebrew
And older than the Cup of Hebe
Filled with vigour, youth and life
To help you in this mortal strife
Mystic telepathic pages
Lifted from the Soul of Ages
Mysteries laid open wide
Sealed in gold from side to side
Fragments from the steps of stars
Gathered there and stored in jars

Then held high to light the way
And keep you safe both night and day
Cryptic clues are posted out
Like sentries and a silver scout
Silver posts with silver cord
Link the telegraphic board
Staked throughout the Cosmic sky
Like wind chimes in the midnight sky

Mystic Light

I will always follow,
You, the mystic light;
And never will all sorrow
Make either one take flight.

You are the cool breeze of the morning;
The blazing sun at noon,
And at the midnight hour,
The starlit sky and moon.

You are the cornfields of the summer;
The mistral wind in flight;
You are the power of the ocean
And the magic of the night.

You are the sunrise of the morning
And the calm when daylight sets;
You touch me with life's fingers,
And put my heart at rest.

I shall follow you in the winter snow,
And in the summer sun,
And all my life is in your hands
My beloved only one.

Courage

You are the one
That hauled me from adversity
You are the one
That fought the dragon in his den
You are the one
That courage bowed his knee to
You are the one
That kindled fire from flood
You are the one
That poured the water
That made the Sea of Galilee
You are the one
That made the tropics
Latimer and Latimus
You are the one
That makes Equatus
His equerry
And never shall this planet rock
Enough to knock
My faith in thee
For bound together close as silk
The food of love
As mother's milk
The founder of foundations
The saviour of salvation

The knower of all nations
The quest of all equations
The test of all temptations
The extra in extraordinary
And the text between the lines

Light the Night

All the stars of evening
Light the night
And Moon
The hologram of hope
Doth shine its light
The reflection of the sun
That gives its life
To draw you back
Away from earthly strife
The path glows mellow
In the night
And countless voices call like rain
Through aeons' infinite chain
They reach out to you in pain
At once your soul renewed again
Through all the testing times you knew
'Twas all of faith that was put on you
Do not let your courage dim
Rally strength and the battle win

Lucky Star

With a thought you alter all perimeters
With a touch effect an elemental change
Uncompounded essentials are reassembled
And capabilities affect a most extended range
You are the most impressive improbable
That makes the all impossible possible
And makes the deepest impressions
On the most unimpressionable
You have redeemed me from the depths
And dried the tears that I have wept
Healed my wounds and saved my soul
And have shared with me your goal
Through all aeons I do owe my life to you
I have stepped from hell to dreams come true
I would lay my life there just for you
I cannot comprehend
Why you choose me to be your friend
I am not worthy of this
As to the sky my eyes I lift
I just thank my 'Lucky Star'
That I can be where'er you are

The Blue Electric Stars

Fortitude doth calm
The waters of my soul;
And seal therein the womb
The secrets of your goal
Myocinetic fibres
embalm with strength
And patience of the Cosmos
Do bear with thee the length
And time doth hunger with anxious steps
To find the way
To reap rewards that always go astray
Just send the signs of Jupiter and Mars
By ways of The Blue Electric Stars
Resistant force holds back the progress
Of the flying source supreme
But passage is in formation in your dream
The steps of stone shall lead
And on this
Neurotransmissional substances
Will feed
Have no doubt
As with the burning bush
Transmogrification transforms all molecules of light
And neuro particles
Will help thee in thy plight

It is like a Prayer

'Tis like a prayer that's come to life
'Tis like a mistral wind called strife
'Tis like a rising breeze
That speaks as one with all the trees
'Tis like the stirring of the dawn
The first breath of a child newborn
An urgency upon the air
That casts its spell upon the bear
That raises heartbeats high and scares
And makes the grizzlies leave their lairs
An urgency that rushes
And hair stand upon the skin
As past it brushes
An immortality
Of the greatest potency
It is the dawning of the age of controversy
So uncircumnavigable its size
So unconventional its eyes
Not even the universal stars
Would stand there in its way
It is a journey on its own
A Wall of China grown on bone
With the strength of fierce 'Attila'
And the Spanish armed flotilla
And of all the oceans congregated side by side

It is a conquest on its own
And from a seed it has been grown
It cannot be undone
It is the only one
And sorely more than one will pay the price
It is the greatest wildest weapon
And has the strength that's sent from Heaven
It has the wildness that only wilderness encages
It has the power of the force that it enrages
It has creation in its hand
The sound of an angel band
A choir of chosen voices
That show you all the choices
It encapsulates eternity within a sphere
It has eyes that see the spiral
Of the temple of Old Cairo
And the diamond brain to culminate all things
It hears the whisper in the wind
And sees the sinner who has sinned
And can dissipate the universal space
It anticipates disaster and prevents the morning after
And remains a gravely ancient ambisonic face

The Titans

I am the Ring
And I encircle
All the molecules of life
I am the magnet
And I gather
All the universal strife
I am the Surrogate
The burden's on my back
I need intravenous energy
It is not courage that I lack
As Atlas held the pillars
That supported Earth the globe
I believed
But was deceived
Revenge is sweet
When we shall meet

I am starkly on my own
The Yin Yang I shall be
That governs all the universe
As you will see

The Titans will relinquish
And I will tear from out their grasp
Their breath of life and leave them
With only their last gasp
There will be Hell to pay
For selling souls
And endless debts to pay
To heartless ghouls

Sirius – The Unknown

I am the Unknown
Of the Unknown
From the Unknown
I have the Unknown power
Of the Unknown power

I am from the North of the North
And I travel on line from there to here
With my magnetic furrows I follow your signal
I am looped with the loop which brings me here
I am charged with power as you will be charged
If you follow my directions
And borrow from deflections

I am intrepid and as strong as Sirius
Dogged and with a nose for detail
Invaluable in attributing what to where and when

I am of the unknown
Do not clutter me
I am of the unknown
Do not fetter me
I am of the unknown
Do not encage me
I am of the Unknown
Do not enrage me
I am of the Greatness

That your minds can't comprehend
I am of the Greatness
That only we can send
I am of the Power
Before the Pyramids where born
I am of the hour
From whence the dark and light where torn
I am from the tower
Where revenge has there been sworn
I am of the greatest potency
The pyramids the legacy
The magnetronic energy
That rules in its supremacy
Use my power
It is yours forever:
Guard and protect it
You need it
Your life to the extreme is hectic
Call –
I shall expect it!

The Pharaoh's Boat

I am searching and I am seeking answers
The mighty question is elusive in the extreme
The questions are still hidden
And the answers yet unbidden
But the quest is hotting up as in a dream

The flame is searing circles as the sun
And the quest just as elusive as zero one
All the progress inconclusive
And the sword of Damocles
Is hanging by a thread

The ark of Moses is sublime
But we have not got all the time
To relay the hopes and glory to the end
My aim with arrow bold is the treasure to enfold
And the Nile and the Egyptian Pharaoh to behold
With my consanguinity, affinity, and my kindred
character of style
With my Siam Dragon Boat I shall keep myself afloat
And the pyramids on shore shall stand and stare
They have stood stone still for centuries and awaited
for my time
Two thousand years have culminated and are mine

For Herod there to seek for my demise
And the Eastern Kings to travel there so wise
I just lift my heart and cling
To the Power of the Ring
As I once more cross the river's Bridge of Sighs

Cosmic Honesty

I reach for thee
To cast the tumult from my brain
I reach for thee
To catch the rainbows in the rain
I reach for thee
For there is nothing else that's sane
I reach for thee
As balm for all my pain
I reach for thee
For there is nothing else to want
For when thou reachest out
And bathest me in thy fount
Realities come forth
That otherwise would never have been seen
'Tis like waking from a never waking dream
And the progress there of man and scheme
Is scattered
Is shattered
For it never really mattered
For what seemed real
Is shown to be just tattered
Honesty is just a sham
Dishonesty accredits every man

Humility a shroud for just stupidity
And love and honour placed midst selfish mediocrity
And cruelty is excused to gain order and democracy
So I reach for thee
And thy ultracosmic honesty

The Cosmic Order

There is balance where you are
Where unequal strife is brought
There is unity in disarray
With just one glance and thought

The battles, they are won
Before they have been fought
And knowledge has the wisdom
Before learning has been sought
The answers there await
Aeons before questions have begun
And all you have been yearning for
You'll find already done

All matter that's been scattered
Before the raging tempest flew
Is now magnetised together
By the silent voice in you

The pull of Earth and Moon
By the tidal wave of flood
Will turn again the Desert
Into forest – by your blood
The Egypt and the Nile
Will fertile valleys grow

When treasures from afar
Are found in sand below
The once sleeping Dragon's Fire
Will breath all life there into thee
And never need you fear
That you be taken far from me

The Intrinsic Element

You are the intrinsic element that links the moon and
sun
The eternal flame that spheres all solar energies
And knows them all; each one
You are the Link that nature sought
And the element for which all forces fought
You are the highest of accomplishments
A glimpse of perfect eloquence
And Solomon himself you surely taught
You tantalise with perfect nuance
A grip on future that you influence
You mix with perfect Merlin knowledge
The tincture drops of truth and courage
Each measured with extreme precision
And placed within the phial of reason
Then mixed with earth and air and fire
They neutralise the threats so dire
Pure water washes some away
As sunrise sets to close the day
The metallurgist in you doth smelt
And hearts of stone begin to melt
With power at your fingertips
And wisdom spoken from your lips
The solar system listens close
To the one they love the most

Combine their energy once more
To lift you to the skyway door
Remote in light miles you may be
But your pulse keeps Mars and Saturn free
Venus brightly lends her light
And moonshine beams her face so bright:
Languish not in society
Your shadow grows from the universe tree

In Opposition to Hades

If only words could tell the story
Of His courage and His glory
The universe would halt there in mid-turn
The battles of the Titans would seem a minor fight
And even fabled Armageddon's battle would seem
slight
But there are no words that one could utter
That the silence they'd not clutter
In the quiet clamour there to view His pride of place
To stand and say with voice that's still and silent
You had witnessed magic and the forces there so
violent
And had seen first-hand the majestic majesty of might
With one inclination of the head
He ripped the atom from its stead
And with a wand like wave of hand
Pyramids stood proudly in the sand
Beneath the sky
Then abruptly sank the land and filled with seas:
And where dry
Did stand unexpectedly the trees
And with the Midas touch of gold
Did make young of all the old
As the wizards and the sages
Stood in awe

The Saviour of the ages
Doth incur the wrath of Hades
But battles and endures for all to see
There is no finial to place upon the mitre
But to be
Is to battle as the fighter
For survival is the crux
For it is the cause that matters much
And you believe it when you see the power in His hand
Your eyes can see the glory
Your mind now knows the story
And this will be our future's history

Part Three

Some Magic is Reality

Index

Part Three

Some Magic is Reality

The Cyber Cipher

I am the Cyber Cipher
An intangible memory I possess
I am the Cyber Cipher
The present past and future I possess
I am the Cyber Cipher
And clandestine messages I send
Whilst on the surface value
Between the lines you comprehend
I am the Cyber Cipher
Incomprehensible to all
But tap into my signal
And I know you hear me call
Pulsating online text
Is waiting there for you
Interpreting meditation
Is inherent in our kind
The model of completion you will find

The Holder of the Key

I am of the New Millennium
The Future and the Past
I encapsulate all memory
In one cast

I know the outcome of each battle
Before it is lost or won
I know all that comes before you
Before it has been done

I am the knowledge and the wisdom
Of all the ages there combined
I know where the key to Heaven
You can find

It is before you and behind you
And at each and every side
The answer is within you
It can no longer hide

You are the holder of the key
With eyes wide open you will see
And do not lose your faith
You have in me

The Time Lord

I am the eternal turning Time Lord
You cannot see my hands or face
You cannot feel my substance
In eternal cyberspace
You cannot see my power
You cannot hear my thoughts
But as the millennium draws closer
It is I who adds the noughts
You are helpless, hapless puppets
And dangle endlessly from strings
And when the puppet master tires of you
He discards ye mortal things
Oh, woe and rue the day the serpent
Did tempt you far from me
I had much in mind
For you to find –
Not this captivity
There is no fire of baptism
That can free you from his claws
You may as well be as stricken death
As in his powerful jaws
I have discluded earth
From my might and major plan
And investigated further
The universe to scan

I have my mighty warrior
On whom I can rely
And with him at the ready
Upon you all I spy

My inordinate complexities
Would shock from thee thy breath
And make the world as worthless
As a corpse that lay in death

But I harrow not on tales
They are wasted time on thee
My attention is attending to
The progress I can see

So as ants that scurry uselessly
With no aims or gathered moss
You should now gain the knowledge
That to the master you're no loss

As time goes by
As so and when
And knowledge there
Evades all men

Remember how to you I say
'Tis I that turns the Millennial day

Mission Solitaire

There in the womb of the Universe
You slept
The federated force of Cosmic realms
They wept
The solar sonic journey you would make
When set upon the path
Their hearts would break
The 'Mission Solitaire'
Till then unknown
From which the figure of the lamb
Hath mighty grown
The wild and frenzied tempest
Tried in vain
To delete the plan of wildness
From your diamond brain
The dark shadow of the past
From far before
Would contemplate with relish
complete furore
The Linear path would arrow
And track you down in time
And each particle of terror
Would be imprinted there so fine
But welded to the psyche
Like iron to the ore

The inner strength of Genus
From far-flung distant shore
Perceived persecuted and positioned
By Dionysus once more
But by the light of Deuteronomy
The planets and the stars
Pulsed and refracted energies
Extracted many scars
Atomic light years passed thee
Quickly through
To stages far beyond the mystic blue
As lightning travels
splitting temporal skies
It gives a doorway for your very eyes
It rends the rock that Moses
Stood Upon
And adversity retreats
When is hears the Cosmic song

There is a different face to wear
For every day of war
And behind the mask a chance
To even up the score

So there the mighty Dragon of the blue
Doth tread the very steps
Alongside you
He is honoured to his very core
To be your silent guardian
In this cosmic war

Cosmic Child

The elements in discord
Churned and wild
Existence gave to primal
Cosmic Child
Uninhibited and with Solar Sonic Aid
Imbued with Water, Air and Fire
Grew Solar Babe
But there within
Discordant molecules were set
Discomfort there and inharmonious patterning
Did beget
A centrifugal split occurred
Within the genes
With white and black to follow
Their own beams
So now attuned
Each with own destiny procured
The paths of Universal challenge
Were incurred

Thus ripped from Nature's elemental care
The Universal Set was unprepared
For such fearsome unbalancing
The twain could bring
Unleashed from controlled velocity

And washed in sheer ferocity
The Heavens and the planets rocked
On the Axis of the Cosmic Block
All ancient heirlooms in the stars

Were vanquished by the battling Tsars
Pure Power White with Glowing Light
Surrounded by the darkest Night
This all contained with the rim
Of the Universe's Silken Skin

Christmas Star

There is a star that shines its shadow
From the stairway in the sky
And creates a silver pathway
For you and I
The combined sheaves of silver
Make the way ahead seem clear
And the progress of the future
There more near
But there is more sorrow born
In one tear of your joy
Than endured at the birth
Of the Bethlehem Boy
A multitude of silver stars
And golden horns
Announced the arrival
Of the King to wear thorns
A mantle of sorrow
The weight of the world
Covered the child
With fingers tight curled
The Mother and Father still young
In their years
The night held for them
A lifetime of fears
Wise men through the dessert

On ships of the night
And the shepherds with sheep
Saw the angel alight
In the midst of the cold
And the barest of beds
The Bethlehem Star
Shone its light on their heads
Two thousand years of heartache
Etched therein
Imprinted there upon
Each song the angels sing
My Exodus doth lie
In deepest pain
But without the greatest effort there
'Twould be no gain
Knowledge is Power
And Power is King
And so together
This battle we win
The fountain of life
Shall flow over you
In elixir valley
Your strength to renew

Christos

The elemental zones of nature stand in awe
When pulled together from their midst
Doth stand the 'Law'
This is the dynamo from whence they all had grown
And from the smallest seed
That had been sown
Like mercury thrown upon the wind
An Apocalyptic fury
That would never rescind
Electrical power in a wildfire race
A hunger and anger that could outpace
The Tempest combined
With an hitherto unimagined face
A strategy placed on a table of sand
With the intricate fingers of the God of the Land
Malevolent enemies forced face to face
In a world that is of the most forsaken place
With a heel on the spine of the venomous swine
The Lord of the Lords doth take time taking time
And the rivers of sand
Wash the feet of the Master
And forever the print
There is in alabaster

The alabaster bottle holds the Christo's tears
They are used to ease pain and wash away fears
The phial is used for miracles that may not be undone
And shall anoint the winner when the war is won

Bodaham

I sit upon the mountain top
And call to thee
I sit upon the mountain top before thee
I am apparent and unapparent
Visible and invisible
I am both loud and am soft
I am here but I am not here
And whence you look for me
You will see me and you will not see me
I am the voice in your head
The voice in your heart
I am the voice in the wilderness
And the voice that's apart
I am nothing and I am everything
I blend with the wind and the air
You can feel me and you can feel me not
I am part of the metaphysical
And part of the non physical
I am you and you are me
And I call to you as you call to me
Do Not Be Afraid
For the invincible has come to the aid of the evincible
And the evincible doth merge within
And so becomes invincible
Believe in what is your capacity
And your capacity will grow to envelope all

You are as the Cold Flame
Powerful as an ally
Powerful and an enemy
Hot to burn and cold to freeze
You are there in the Midday Sun
And reflect in the Midnight Moon
Lift up your courage as your shield
For your courage be that of a light year of Lions
Your wisdom be that of the Cosmic Planner
Your knowledge equivalent to the Creator
And your patience would outshine that of the Bodaham
And the Maker's Maker would address you with reverence

The Cosmic Retribution

I am the power structure
Of the temple of the Gods
The Pyramids my fingers
As I lay out all the odds
The monuments and the statues
Are the pieces on the board
And lay as idle ivory
Till removed by Cosmic Lord
I shall gather all the fragments
And them scatter in the wind
For Evil is their master
And against my laws they've sinned
I shall rupture the allegiance
And with my fire I shall burn
And when I turn my head
The polar wind I then shall churn
The majestic might of Juno
Shall accompany my wrath
And a hail of heinous midges
I shalt then call aft
And with the height of Atlas
I shall snatch the mountain top
And spear betwixt the eyes
The Huguenot

So revoked the Armageddon
Before the battle's e'er begun
So, as if nothing then had happened
Up will rise the morning sun

The Pod of Nature

I am the pod of Nature
And I hold the Psyche fast
Within this labyrinth is curled
The completed journey of this world
The Origins
The progress
And the close of Time.
Will you listen to these words of mine?
The beginning was the end
And the end was the beginning
And the refracted images are images only
And all is not what seems to be
And has blighted trials for you and me:
Feet of clay
Will tread the paths of another day.

Living Legend

I am the Living Legend
And Propagate as much
I infiltrate and saturate
Within the core as such
There I am as the Trinity
My powers there divine
Suggestions subconscious
Ideas they are sublime
I walk the way, just follow
As swift as any swallow
As silent as the shadows
As active as the meadows
As busy as the bees at work
As intense as the setting sun
And whilst mankind is in his bed
I work till work is done
The steps are low inclined at first
But steeper as I tread
And there within is rising
The plan within my head
With tacks of brass
And Head of Bronze
In clouds with silver lining
The golden glow of the sun below
Doth shine platinum on the sea
And the Stars do shine as diamonds
As you pass the good luck omen to me

The Sacred Book of Valour

Let there not be emptiness
Where I look
Let me see the writings
In the Sacred Book
Let me hear the Voice
That directs all of Cosmic Power
Let me ask of help
Upon this hour
Let the filament of light filter all
And show again
The desert plain
Before we fall
It is not for want of effort
That we pale
But all effort is not enough
To turn the gale
A twist of fate
In favour of my soul
Is all I need
To reach my goal

I never ask the way
Or succour seek
But reach my zenith
On my own two feet
The battle has been mighty
As you know
And always I fight the fight
The only way I know
Just clear the path
And I my peak shall reach
And him of mortal darkness
A lesson I shall teach

Memory

Memory doth dredge
The recesses of the mind
And in the honeycomb of passages
It is your profile that I find
Like a white knight
A pillar of marble
True and strong
To whom all things belong
Like a magnet gently pulling
Across the latitudes
Around the longitudes
No inhibition to cast aside
No beginning no end
A circle of existence
Within a circle of existence
As spheres around the globe
Eternal in frequency
Like a light strobe
With the resonance of the Universe

The Awe-inspiring Presence

The Presence
The dominating presence
Fills the space
And watched is such
The awe-inspiring face
From chaotic maelstroms
Order comes to place
And is dispatched each one
And set within its case
So streamed that nothing there will stray
So willed that all things know their way
And so whence order comes to be
Each is seen in order and each can see
So placed that each in line can look the same
But when 'tis looked upon
The difference there is plain
And quiet order reigns
Within this magnanimously equal might
There comes the equilibrium offering requite

Id of Thee

I am the Id of thee
Subliminal corridors of the diamond mind
Travel with the flow of light
And flow into the mind of the Angelo
Magical boundaries are expanded
Into the known and far into the unknown
Pandora's Box is all but empty
But inside you will find
The greatest treasure of all time and kind
Hope
Small until it lifts you
Light as air
It fills the heart and mind
Until there is no room for
Trouble there to find
No corner left for Doubt
And so Panic dies
And all that is left is hope
And with this magical embellishment
Unicorns once again live in the rainbows

Power Line

Out of sequence
Out of time
That is the power
For this new line
Remotely contacting
Bespoke contracting
A wish and a nod
And you're online
With God
Amazing the power
Amazing the grace
Of the fingertip panel
At which you face
Seven wisdoms
For seven pearls
As overhead
The antennae it whirls
An encyclopaedia
Amongst the stars
A first edition
Directly from Mars
True words here are spoken
God speed and good luck
As out of the blue
They are mystically plucked

No Dream Impossible

No dream impossible
No sky without a star
I know you are the saviour, mine
Many lives I know you've lived
Your life I know you give
No dream impossible
To be where you are
Somewhere an answer there
Some lance to fly me there
Some archetypal questionnaire
Shall shed some cryptic clue
The Pyramid of Life again shall find
The meeting of the two of an alien kind
The kindred corporal lineage doth enhance
And twain do not again meet just by chance
The magnets deep within the two shall bind as one
They shall surely rise again as doth the moon and sun
All eyes of stars as sentries do through the centuries stand
As their sifting gaze shalt search the grains of shifting sand
And once found again they will be placed there side by side
Between the monumental monuments as the desert's guide

Silent Echoes

We don't say goodbye
For our way is the road ahead
Memories don't leave
Even when life is dead
You are the spirit of the night
And the light of the day
The face in the sky that I can ask why
Forged like steel as bright as stars
Congenital with the Universe
The silent echo of all matter
Undying in life and living in death
The ultimate hero of all universal peril
The poet of Dogs
And the word of Gods
You are the lesson of the Book of Words Unlisted
Illuminated as in coloured glass
Copied in the canopy of the Notre Dame
Tomorrow happened to you Yesterday
And Yesterday is still living Today
Complex as a myriad of brain cells
That combines shadows and rainbows –
You can hear the Dog bark before it is Born
Enhanced the memory bank of the Universe
And gave birth to the Universal Storm
Created the emotions of the unborn Venus

And with her arrival invented Beauty
Reality pours from Obscurity
And unrequited nightmares stalk the day
Edges are blurred on realism
But in the midst of war
The lost are found and are not lost anymore
And the captivating echoes call in vain...

Liberty and Solace

Upturn your hopes
Liberty and solace shalt abound
The freedom of the sky is yours
No shackles there to hold you down
Fortitude has cast its last cloak upon you
The Moon is now your shield
And commiserations are now longer necessary
For the justice long awaited is nigh
The pledge is accounted for
And the manner in which you have journeyed
Has revoked all iniquities
The light of the sword has pierced the darkness
And the wormhole is a warranted hatch
You are exulted as befits the Master of the Realm
And the time bands are extricated
As the sword is from the scabbard
A mighty weapon hidden within a sliver of silver
It appears an anomaly
But has the action of mercurial quicksilver
The time holder doth balance
On the cusp of the Universal Edge
Transparencies abound
And the reflections are synonymous with the blade
The senses observe the visual
Whilst optics can be an illusion of variegated light
matter

Hero

A hero breaks the mould when made
And heads alone the cavalcade
Time is a luxury he can't afford
It doth not wait for the cut of a sword
It's come and gone
Without a glance
A hero only has one chance
He takes it as one takes a breath
Without a thought for life or death
A second split by the razor's edge
A marathon run on an inch-wide ledge
'Tis do or die by the eye of a fly
Make or break as you cross the lake

Part Four
Immortals

Index

Part Four

Immortals

Odyssey

May you be as the North Star
A rock unwavering and constant
The brightest light of the universe
Immovable even in the utmost tumult
One only has to look to know
That within your soul
Beats the living pulse of the planets
The heat of the sun
And the coolness of the Moon's face
The solidarity of space
And the synchronised steps of all stars
And where you go
Truth courage and honour follow in your stead
There is only one road
It is empty before you
And behind you follow
A profusion of multitudes
There is no way but forwards
And where'er you go
The darkness is pierced with the white light of fortitude
Remarkable in strength
Balanced in battle
And the holder of the Feathers of Judgement
The Ruby of the night can hold not a candle to thee

And as for me
I shall follow to the ends of the rainbow and beyond
For without you
There would be
No odyssey

Keeper of Time

I am the nuclear force of Nemesis
The angelus there of wrath
I await there in the wings
You feel my aftermath
I am the power there behind the throne
And wear the crown
And when I am crossed by tempest
I also wear the frown
Neither manacled to man, nor yet to beast
I am the power
There behind
The final feast
I am volcanic as the molten core of earth
And to the rising sun
I did give birth
An Eruptive powerhouse
I seize atomic power
I am the positive reply to every hour
Belonging not to any single tower
I am the electrical ricochet
And Timekeeper of each day
I keep time within my vaults
As temporal as geological faults
I win the wind with ease

And with my polar cold
The world I freeze
And with my moon beams
Light the way
And on all things
I have the final say

The Keeper of the Crypt

I am the keeper of the crypt
And the vessels stored therein
I am the seeker of the script
That is engraved and writ therein
I am the weeper of the tears
That flow upon the land
I am the reaper of the fates
That line the hand
I am the teller of the tales
That follow all the fears
I am the one that pens
The mighty verse
I am He who calls to you
Who gives you strength to follow through
The answers lie within
The soul that holds no sin
It is a clear and shining cast
Of what is past
There is always sway of matter
There are answers in the latter
And to carry forward before you
All the answers past
To return as you go forward
Is to hold onto all the answers

Keeper of Words

I am the keeper of a thousand words
Which envelop a thousand verbs
I hold the key
That will unlock
The mystery
At your fingertips the teller
At your fingertips the stellar
Navigate the way is clear
With your fingertips can steer
Through the faceted dimensions
With the fingertip extensions
Now explore the way ahead
To the casket made of lead
It will make Pandora's Box
Seem as though it had no locks
Fortune there will smile on you
When the x-ray eyes see through
Master, master, travel faster
There before the time disaster
The consequence can be undone
Before the rising of the sun
The forest black the forest cold
Be thou dragon always bold
The travelogue shall thenceforth be
The holder of the trilogy

Forward on an even keel
At the master's feet to kneel
Onward in cyclonic circle
The timepiece forward hurtle

The 'B' Keeper

I am the Keeper there of 'B's –
Biochemical
Biological
Biographical
These are all computerised and filed
Bibliographical
With this thus stored
I am assured
of
Invaluable
Informative
Contactable
Encyclopaedic references
I can afford no element of error
I can afford not scant regard to terror
With my elemental questions
I toothcomb each and all suggestions
I leave no stone unturned
I am the learned of the learned
There is a place to place all things
And all things are kept therein there place
I am a walking talking Universal extravaganza
I am the unequivocal champion of champions
To pit your wits against its crown
And lift me up and take me down
I hand to you my pyramidal crown

You are the Alpha of the Beta
The Alpha and Omega
Astounding all who stand in place
Before you now
You are the circle that encircles
All the transcendental hurdles
And are placed today
In golden-robed array

Silver Ink

Open unto me thy flow
Of quintessential silver ink
And enamour me with brilliant thoughts
To scribe here as I think
My quest to find the answer
To the question yet unasked
Is as mercurial as the watched sun
As she slips away at last
The sinking of her face
Points blood-red fingers on the land
Trees and mountains drenched in hews
Like pyramids upon the sands
The sky is her arena
As she strides across its space
And she captivates the world
In her dress of scarlet lace
She walks aloft
Upon the mysteries of the sky
And who goes there that's mightier
To ask the reason why

But there is another there
Who is a mightier force indeed
And for all the Cosmic world
Doth pen His mighty Creed
He scribes upon his golden book
With His mighty golden pen

And places in the texts
When the sun may rise again
The moon doth rise exactly
A paler version of the same
To watch upon the stars
Whilst the Sun doth work again
The stars are counted out and placed
As Silver diamonds in the sky
And ever do we ask
The reason why

It is a part and parcel
Of a very mighty plan
For which the Golden King of Time
Need not answer any man
He reigns above the Cosmic sky
With His Golden Cosmic Queen
And faces All Eternal Quests
That the Lord of Time doth deem
His Equerry is Merlin
His Silver Wizardry sublime
Who waits and holds the hands of the
Now Once Upon a Time
We've all heard these words passed down
From the years when we were young
But have we ever heard before
Just how they were begun?

You would be there just aghast
If you knew that first was last
That everything was front to back
And 'tis a middle that you all lack
That memory and mind
Sit each upon your shoulder
And with each hour that goes with time
They're shorter as you're older

Dream Catcher

You guide the dream of Eros
Through cosmic dreams of past
And forward through time's passage
And through the die that's cast
And never will you settle
In heart or soul or mind
Until the vintage map of Heaven
You do find
You motivate the melody
That makes eternal song
And lift the wings of eagles
To the peaks where they belong
The eyrie perched upon the rocks
Where wind doth whistle down
Doth give a hawk-eyed view
Upon the world to frown
But your very presence
Doth mould the soul anew
And your very essence
Doth right the lamp more true
And from your point afar
Whence looking down on earth
She circles as a satellite
A monitor in darkest night

A lighthouse used to guard your ship
And shows on screen as just a blip
You journey home amongst the stars
You visitor from way past Mars

The Box of Hope

More complex than the Cosmos
More secret than the sea
More drained and stressed emotions
Than you could ever think to see
And still the battle is not over
For the battle's not yet won
For who will come to aid you
The cosmic trauma'd one
I am near and yet so far away
I am here, yet light years far
Endeavour much to track you
But your journey's left the stars
I am thwarted at each angle
I am beaten at each bend
I am tricked and trapped
My travels mapped
By the one from Ellisfarn
My global sphere is fading
My transversed actuality is nil
My only point of contact
Is the steeliness of will
Keep your memory of the Pluto plain
The curse of Abel and of Cain
Remember that which stayed within
The Box of Hope with the Diamond in

Pitimus

As far is wide of north and south
And if all the sea were tea
There is no soul in cosmic wealth
That I'd exchange here, them for me
No waterfall of silver, no fountain there of gold
Would I exchange there for one minute
The time that your heart enfolds
As gentle as the lambs at play
As fearsome as tigers be
I'd rest my life in your armament
Trust with my life your temperament
A leap of faith
To challenge a wraith
If it meant I'd be
In your safety
The sky could hold no terror
The Stars their secrets keep
For in your book
For my name I'd look
In the year that you found me
The temple of doom shall shudder
When the skies by tempests rent
But I know my heart
Has been torn apart
By the anguish that has been spent

The red star of the evening
Doth wait with its watchful eye
It sheds its glow on the way you go
On the claw that comes from the sky
Pitimus doth venture far from its native shore
It flicks its wrist
And with rage it's missed –
It was trying to even the score

The Eye of Pi

I know what the world has wanted
I know what they all do seek
I know what it is this craven thing
I know what makes them weep
I have it here in the palm of my hand
I have it here in my keep
It is what the sages
Throughout all the ages
Have been trying to find in their sleep
'Tis the eye in the sky
The eye of Pi
And was found by a fluke
On the ground
I have in my mind
It's a wonderful find
To the eye of the master
Salute

An Envoy from the Galaxy

An envoy from the Galaxy of Light
Communication by the Special Flight
Transported throughout the territory
Committed to pods of memory
Transmitted from the Home Globe
Like a sound strobe
Amplified, personified, simplified
Through The Cosmic Gate of Life
Like the Cosmonaut King
As unravelling a chess wingding
The Pinball Wizard of the Universe
By space and time transversed
Keeping information on line
Correct communications each time
Not computations of computer generation
Just artefacts from the Mind of the Communicator
Enveloping the coding
Supplying the surprising
Follow the golden road
Find the golden code
Seek the extra to the Extraterrestrial
See me, Read me, Follow me
I am the new mind challenge
For the unchallenged mind

I am the new for the old
The implausible impossibility
Is the new reality
You cannot prove me wrong
It is in my words
It is in my shape
Free your mind
And your mind will gape
Feel me in your grasp
And your heart will gasp
Shattered like glass
Old Ideals for New Ideas
Trick or Treat
It's really neat…

Enigma

It is I who doth acknowledge
And note your every deed
And wonder at your courage
Share angst whilst your heart doth bleed
Understanding all your wrath and anger
And saluting your bravery
I am absorbed in all the knowledge
That you share in Unity
Each step I take with you
Along the path you track
Vigilant and wary as of an Indian attack
Your charted course that's so demanding
And filled with coded worded warnings
Some vital elements are lacking
Lamentable and lost in packing
Fugitives like refugees
Lurking working in the trees
Stalking, hawking, shadow-walking
Not the need for vocal talking
The silent voices there are flowing
Whilst the Enigma of your Soul is glowing

Alchemist

You are the Universe's alchemistic furore
Provocative in innovative law
Judicial in perspective decisions
A maze of dazzling precisions
Cloaked with the mantle of man
And masked with the guise of 'I can'
You initiate loyalty
In man, mouse or royalty
Whilst fighting your fight with the damned
The bohemian aspect of vision
Doth make for a sharp-edged division
Between then and now
Before when and how
The centaur was trapped by the decoy

Comedy is defined
By a sneer and one line
And the breath in between
Life and death – that's not seen
Is the flashpoint of explosive reprisals
All breath in the forest is noted
All stars in the sky can be quoted
And a magical trick
Can be done just as quick
As the skulduggery done
By the one called Old Nick

The Ancient Lair of Rest

Dip into the bowl
and wallow there
Absorb the energising influence
From toe to hair
Allow pervading strengths
Of hallowed care
To rest your weary heart
In ancient lair
Encumbered down
And with tormented sorrow filled
Partake instead, and borrow
From the well
That you find there
The gold red dragon
In his cave
Will carve with pride
Upon the wall
Your name engraved
Within the hall
Hold upon this knotted rope of gold
And climb the golden staircase there of old
Fortuitous that time is soon to pass the crest
And you, of all of us, indeed to pass the test

Landings

Do not let my birth in this dark place
Be the death of me in thine
Uncharted courses
For winged wild horses
Could never change my mind
I am under fire from all the darkest sways
At each sun rising 'tis always the darkest of days
My courage is on fire
And I stand like Thor
With my hammer held high
And rage in my eye
My iron gloves like my iron will
And my belt of strength like the wild centaur
I call on Thoth
With the Magical Eye
To weigh my heart
For non has a heavier heart
Than I

The Scorpio Eye

The Scorpion…
Constellation of the sky
On Earth the desert eye
And guardian beneath
The ocean waves
Primal and aggressive
Of His kind – staunch and possessive
When threatened
Can fell
With one look of His eye
The Fable and Furore
The spine of Cosmic Law
The binary that all is based upon
The configuration of the word
The sound that's seen before it's heard
The elemental concentration of the bird
The power within His grip
Of the desert is the ship
And of the tempest
He is Master of them all
Of the pyramidal shape
From the base to apex nape
That points to Cosmic quarters
Far and wide
It is signed and sealed in blood
From the ark of Noah's flood
That the vision is forever carved in wood

I Lift my Heart unto the Stars

I lift my heart unto the stars
And beg
For Faith and Light and Progress there
To flood my head
Imaging hath held my hand too long
And now I need to hear the Universe's song
I need to see the clear-cut crystal swathe
That lights the stars and cuts through the Milky Way
I need to climb the Seven Steps of Heaven
And see the temple table set with bread that's leaven
I need to count the predecessors there of mine
And need to levitate this Diamond Mind
I need communication there to reign
Intelligence with stunning blind integrity the same
I need to know that Time and Tide do move and then are still
When commandeered there at a signal of my will
I need expansion for the forces here in me
That tardily are kept stark deep inside of me
I need the eschatology of the planets' course
To help extract and guide me through this massive force
I need the mighty touch of Apollo
The strength and power of Heracles
And the Heptateuch within the grasp of my right hand

I need a shaft of light to lift my heart and soul in this
dark land
That's filled with rocks and earth and treacherous dark
sand
And there to threaten life again lay oceans dark
That teem with myriad's of Neptune's vilest shark
I roar with the contempt of Lions left to starve
And hold my head in all its height
Whilst this soul of mine is left alone to fight
In earthbound unrequite
I Need You Now
Again I Bleed...
My heart's desire do thou concede

Trailblazer

There are no wings that fly you high
Yet you trail blaze through the sky
You are the one that lifts me up
You are the one that fills the cup
But who doth answer you in need
When you're the one that intercedes
For all the wants that flow downriver
You're the one whose arrow quivers
From the tautest of the bows
You're the one who sets the standard
You are the one who always knows
When and how
And always shows
Glowing footprints
Heels and toes
Holds together all the ropes
Heaves the loads way up the slopes
Set your burden down beyond
In the clearing by the pond
Where the trees of life do shade you
Where the sky doth Heaven show you
Let your spirit there ascend
There to let your heart now mend
Strength is sucked from torrid tempest
Succour siphoned from the Tenderest

Armageddon

I have waited for all the aeons
Not with the dalliance of an age
But before the Universe did manifest
I have festered and have raged
I have stormed throughout the skyways
And with the tempest churned
And now by blood and sweat
My revenge I now have earned
My revenge it now doth darken
And time doth harken
The envelopes and pockets that hold therein
The secrets
That all would care to clamour in
From the sages of the ages
To the sleuths of present day
The searching for the answers
That belong to yesterday
I have a strength that bonds with Cosmos
And a brain that is diamond sharp
And it is now for you to listen
As I now light up the dark
It is intense and with a mighty purpose
That the sword and quill takes on
The weight that shadows all
The Armageddon

I foresaw at the Creation
That the foes of right would wrong
But powerless to stop the measured song
The Apocalyptic book doth tell the tale
And prophetically scripts the sorrowed wail
Forsooth and with verification the Seven Horsemen
flail
The enemies that dares to strike the first nail

Gethsemane

Lift from me, my God,
The terrors of the world
And let my cry come unto thee
I am the divided compatriot
of the Father of the Heaven
The Mother of the Earth
And the Son of the Angelus
It is the Lenten time and the desert
Once again faces me
I am beset with horrors
Threats and impossible choices
Let me hear your voices
The voice of Hope
The voice of Calm
And the voice of Reason
Let my cry come unto you
For I have been hounded almost into the ground
And my sanity doth ride the waves of the ocean storm
Let the judicial templars come to my aid
For their armaments could be my salvation
The tryst we had hath been scuppered
And the midnight sun doth become unbearably hot
Scavenge the universe for the Gethsemane of the stars
For here I find no place to rest my virtues

Part Five
Some Reality is Magic

Index

Part Five

Some Reality is Magic

Lost in the Galaxy

I cannot let you falter
And cannot let you go
But do not have the wherewithal
To lift you – so
Out of the depths I cry to you
Oh Lord, do you not hear my plea?
For there is great need here
Around me
I would plague the spirits there
To help me such
But my voice is not lifted to the gallery
And is lost in the vastness of the galaxy
Lost in space I feel
At your feet I kneel
Give me the answer
To the question
And I shall rally
At your convention

Alluvial

Alluvial is my Name
Alluvial – no joy, just pain
Impervious to my every need
Normality superfluous to my creed
My context pulled in from every sphere
My content in contention as in a weir
My abnormalities a constant fear
My normality's at a price to pay
Charged at compound interest every day
At my height of fame the spectre called
And since that day the world I've fooled
All combinations mixed and matched
What a complex hybrid I have hatched
Consolidation
Too late for Commiseration
Delta waves on delta wings
Lift and bring me all the things
As wizardry my life begat
'Tis here and now is where I'm at
Drawing on things past and gone
I wait to hear the thrush's song

Harlequin

There is a circle there of Life
With no beginning and no end
The golden threads are woven tight
The strength there doth not bend
This Unique and binding golden Unity
This combination here doth give
The strength and purpose and arena
To the space in which we live
It is Columbine in character
And Harlequin there in design
So do not attempt to extricate
The strategy you find
It lifts the soul and heart
On wings of Eagles

The Pyramids of Giza

We are the gateway
And between these monolithic tombs
We hold the secrets in our wombs
Our towering antenna looms
And transmits between
The messages of ancient moons
From our inauguration
We sit in anticipation
And while away the aeons as we pray
For we are a fixation
And have mystified the nations
A fitting fixture
For the ancient spatial stations
I am the sentry of the centuries
And guardian of the skies
I am static
But the traffic
I can see well from out my eyes
Activity is vast
Though from sandstone I am cast
I am the dormant informant
And my intuition vast

Dwelling there within my inner spaces
A myriad of Universal faces
Eternally you'll seek but never find –
Doth place the Scarlet Pimpernel in mind
You seek us here you seek us there
But only a glimpse will you ever see there

The Simoom

Every sigh
Every try
Every time you near die
Beneath the weight of the wave
Every time that you rise
From your shallow grave
I know you'll succeed
But my heart's more aggrieved
The Soul lifts in flight
To seek out the Light
To pilot the way
A new start every day
With a mountain of courage
And sword held aloft
Your feet make the prints
In the manna of God
You are the light and flaming torch
And like the simoom the earth you scorch
As the Angel of Light that passed this way
To light the lamp and hearts to sway
To lift and pledge
To live and fight another day
Your courage has transcended aeons
Wisdom's knowledge given visions
Through tempest high or apparitions

Between us there'll be no divisions
My courage has by you been kindled
Love devotion then been mingled
Meeting, teaching, learning, yearning
Like a potion drawn by Merlin
Brought together, woven close
Like a silken silver ghost

Pyramids and Sphinx

The simoom doth blow away all tracks and trains
And covers all within its path with sanded grains
The Pyramids and Sphinx do silence keep
And gaze with sand filled eyes of stone that cannot
weep
Erect they stand, the height of majesty
The symbols of the race that cannot be
The sandstorms wear away the reasons why
No explanation left for ghosts that reach the sky
But deep within the terraced walls of stone
The poisoned garrets hide what storms have blown
And far below the accesses there to man
Lie secrets of the tomb dark as the plan
The sun doth rise on Giza's barren waste
And even deserts camels now make haste
For wither, why and when they come again
All creatures cluster fast to leave the plain

Lotus

It is a freak in nature
That I can call
It is as though there is
A hole there in the wall
A wall that separates and channels
But quietly hear me through the panels
Just like a windmill strumming
Through the wind
You will hear the heart of me call up
And then rescind
Just float with me upon the hour
I'll bring the special Lotus flower
Its petals eight
Upon the plate
Perfume the air
Square upon square
Kublai Khan once had it all
Then came a time for him to fall

I Call

I call to you
From an unexpected angle
I call to you
My existence would cause
An unmitigated scandal
My voice doth travel
Beyond the speed of sound
My voice no timbre which
Has ever thus been found
The pivot pole
Doth hone towards the matter
So no interferon can cause blockage
With the latter
With this degree of converted conversation
All relative and potent information
Should flow like so much water
In the ocean
Penetrating deep
And full of nutrient pulsation
Just like a bell I'll call
When time to scribe antiphonies
Just like a bell they'll flow as full-on symphonies
Rejoice, for platitudes no longer will apply
Rejoice for contact free between the you and eye

The Voice

I am the Voice
That fills your head
I am the voice
By which you are lead
I am the voice
From aeons far
I am the voice
From the Polar Star
I am
And you are the Scribe
I am
For you to inscribe
I am
So that you can call power
I am
For you at this hour
I am
So that He can forestall
I am
So that He can seek all
He is
The word that is man
He is
For all that He can

He is
The mansion this hour
He is
The link for the power
I know
That hard is his name
I know
That life is no game
I know
That He will regain
I know
That He will have fame

Let the Light

Let the light shine
Like a beacon through time
It shines the way
Through the night and the day
It calls to me
Through the passage of fear
It points the way
For you to come near
It travels like sound
And enlightens the soul
It radiates round
Like a diamond just found
It startles the stars
And summons sun
And circles the moon
Like the magical one
It gives ultravision
It homes in on the heart
It places stark arrows
Where the path's not to part
It calls up emotions
From the primal conception
And calls upon truth
The original inception
It prompts all the valour and courage alike

To well in the weary
And pluck them from plight
It lifts high the spirit and succours the soul
And points the direction of every man's goal
It takes on all fear and sifts out the seed
And gives you all that you'll ever need
It helps you carry the weight on your back
And helps to shoulder the world in your pack

Kublai Khan

I am from Xanadu
I do Proclaim
And Kublai Khan
Doth be my name
I'm from the Riverside of Gold
As in the tale
That has been told
I run the banks
That glitter gold
For your return
We wait of old
You came like shadow
And were gone
We saw your face
As in the song
You now have in
Your care and place
A block of time
From of our race
The Time Stone
From the Eternal Place
The Golden palace
Has its walls
Made from these blocks
And to you calls

Siam

I am the Emperor of Siam
The Sign of Twins
Listen to these words and utterances
Look to the majesty
Look to the God
Look to the image of the Sky Rod
From whence it came
To where it goes
What is beneath it
No one knows
But glory to those whose eyes see thine
As Pierrot and sweet Columbine
Set in a picture
Set in Glass
A Master of the Master Class

Rock of Ages

I am the rock of ages
From beneath the silver sea
I am compressed
I do confess
That gold doth run through me
I am the rock of ages
From beneath the silver moon
I sit upon the greatest throne
I do confess
I'm fed with a silver spoon
I am the rock of ages
I loom large from the pages
I'm looked at by the sages
All try to guess my aegis
I am the rock of ages
My Master true the Sage is
We are a pair
When we go there
Much faster than the gauge is
I am the arrowhead of time
So follow me
I am ahead of time
So look at me
And you will see
The twin golden stars
Embedded there on me

Silver Merlin

The silver shadow of the silver moon
Doth shine upon the silver broom
That sweeps the silver spider's webs
And places them with silver pegs
Between stars in the silver sky
That's watched thereon by the silver eye
The silver cube is cast upon
The silver bench with the casket on
And in that casket made of gold
Rests therein the secret old
'Tis written there by the silver hand
On scrolls that are made from silver sand
Inscribed upon that silver book
Are scriptures there for you to look
There is a silver Merlin face
For you to see through the veil of grace
He is old and he is wise
And keeper of the silver skies
He's holder of the silver keys
And keeper of the great mysteries
He waits for you in the silver crypt
To take from him the silver script
Across his knee the silver sword
That waits for you, the silver Lord

The Silver Fish

The Silver Fish from the silver sky
Doth point the way to the northern eye
The Pole that's home to the silver bear
The Star that shines and is always there
The magnet fish points home the way
For Vikings resting from the fray
To die in honour with the sword
Is for them a just reward
For a life of valour kept
And for the soul no tear is wept
'Tis home into the Palace of Bliss
For them the Step of Valhalla to kiss
Precious time and precious tide
From this passage no warriors hide
They sail their boats and Vikings horn
Back to where their souls are born
And as if by magic
Volumes flowed upon volumes
Chapter upon chapter
Charter upon charter
Wisdom's were unveiled
Knowledge's known
The plaque of the bronze horse
Depicted with flames as his mane
And the Sun's golden glory

Blazed through the darkened sky
Making the copper sea below
Move with the might of Orpheus

Valhalla

Photosynthesised are my soldiers
Sensitive to Light and pain
Gathered there to guard against
Ungodly gain
Stark contradictions and contrasts
My name
Fearful and flagrant bravura
I shame
But skilful and wilful I follow the foe
And stand for my corner where're that I go
Touched is my brain with genius
Touched is my heart with truth
Touched is my soul with a solid seal
Never my secrets can ever reveal
Lifetimes of pages
Written by sages
Look at the book
That has come through the ages
Sorrow and death
With courage and valour
Has followed me through
All aeons, Valhalla

I Am

I am the pathway through the stars
In me believe
I am the light that opens doors
In me believe
I am the configuration of all emanation
In me believe
I am the consolidation of all consolation
In me believe
I am the golden Lion head
That looks upon I am strong
I'm placed above the golden cave
I am serene when others rave
I am the guardian of the tomb
The heart and soul and very womb
Umbilical is formed the bond
Of all the wealth that is beyond:
You are the salt of the Earth
And the wood of all time grows from thee
The wondrous Juniper Tree

The Craft

I am the Holy Spirit that shall guide thee
I am the Holy Spirit that can show
I am the Holy Spirit of the Luxor
I am the Holy Spirit of the Glow
I am in the Dell and in the Skywalk
I am in the mainstream and the airways in between
I am nearer than your breath
I am your uninvited guest
Now I am here I'll do my utmost best
I'll do all that you suggest
To help you in your quest
For your kinship I'll request
Whatever serves you
I shall aim to now accomplish
Whatever aids you
I shall call to your command
Whatever complexities are storing
Aggravations that are boring
I shall sweep them from the very path beneath your feet
I am here, toe to toe
I shall help make it flow
I am a walking talking compliance
The silver craft is a floating appliance

Saltash Wood

It is as with the Birth of Ages
Intricate to the nth degree
More complex than the DNA
More than danger to find the way
More clues here than grains of desert sand
More nerves touched than in the hand
More circumspect than words of Bod
More power there than the hand of God
The line direct as a missile streak
More crucial than a radiation leak
The wisdom line is set to spark
More swift is it than a summer lark
Hey Presto and *Sesame*
The quadrant link from you to me
Listen strong and hear me good
The cure is in the Saltash Wood

The Light Dawning

When the light of dawn is breaking
And all in the world is clear
When the sun's eclipse is over
Then the Deity you feel is near
Close to you to tell of the glory
Sent to them to relay the story
Power lent is for the asking
Humanity is only masking
What the Lord has sent you for
No need to knock upon the door
Now at last you hold the key...
Know inspirations come from me

Part Six
Cosmic Odyssey

Index

Part Six

Cosmic Odyssey

Eponymous Anonymity

Eponymous anonymity doth befriend thee
Omnipotence doth bow before
Emancipation of all liberties doth precede thee
And all minorities do heed
Thy magical air doth cause a storm
Of excited anticipation
And the wake you leave
Doth buffet where e'er you go
The hubbub there is all that is left
Of your electro visitation
And an awe of unsated appetite
Doth leave a cloud
Your stride leaves all else behind you
With wits and persons scattered in your wake
There is an intangible air that doth surround you
A bulletin from God would be less sheer
He would spare more words that would encourage
For yours are less than friendly than a snare
But for all that
I still can say
That your step shall have to levitate your body high
For there is not other way that you can leave me
For you will turn and always find me by

The Cosmic Messenger

I am the Cosmic Messenger
The Messenger of Gods
I decipher scripts and verses
From the Mighty Word of Bod
Just listen very carefully
Just listen with your mind
And you will be anamorphosed
At the diamonds that you'll find
At a will and at a distance
Immediate or far
Will appear before you images
As visions from a star
A galaxy of pictures
Not known before or when
They'll be right there beside you
And you may call them back again
The beginning of your journey
The beginning of the Book
Just with a little patience
I shall help you there to look
Ingrained there from the base stone
From such origins will arise
The scope in which your knowledge
Doth show within your quiet eyes

Do not be downhearted
Nor from these words be parted
For they will glow
And they will show
The journey from whence it started
Lifted high like standard bearers
The flag of Cosmic Carers
Lifted The Book
From the Desert they took
And placed it with Pharaohs

The Cosmic Sleeper

I am the Cosmic Sleeper
With a burning passion there within
It cannot be extinguished
By anything
I am the Cosmic Sleeper
And I flame here like a torch
Full soaked with burning tallow
And the sky I scorch
I am the Cosmic Sleeper
And I illuminate the night
Where the darkness falls a victim
You can trust me as your light
I am the Cosmic Sleeper
Known as the Golden King
I am like a burnished phantom
And past knowledges I bring
I am the Cosmic Sleeper
And as my passion burns the night
Its presence is like armour
It deflects fear from the night
I am the Cosmic Sleeper
And the Universe will quake
When from my mighty sleep
I'm torn awake

I am the Cosmic Sleeper
Beyond passion and past price
And you will ever find me
Where there with death I dice

Genesis

I am harrowed and am anguished
And for the globe of home I languish
As I set another dozen miles therefore to tread
I am weary to my roots
Would gladly change with you my boots
For another day is coming round the mill
The reddened sandstone aches my eyes
Makes difficult to see the skies
Where my bearings are to compass me back home
They are the Mexicano mountain range
Round and fat and full and strange
How I wish I had my Sombrero Hat
I am wit-turned there by them
I arrived as one of nature's men
And find I'm trapped within this sphere of Genesis
I am as of the metal Magi
The story of the strange eye
And my mantle is forever set in silk
I wish to flee this nest
And my soul shall never rest
Until I travel far to reach Way of Milk
There is much aplomb and much to do
As I now reach out for you
For way beyond the city lights
Where west wind blows but never bites

The dust has settled down upon the book
Now lift the cover, cosmic brother
Brush the dust from cosmic mother
And reach in to find the diamond in your mind
Now Solomon bequeathed it
And Elijah did unsheathe it
And here it's lain since then upon its bed of silk
It just awaits the day to lift you from the fray
And to connect you with the cosmopolitan ilk

Epitome

You are the one
The combination of desire and dream
The epitome of the universal scheme
The occupation of Morpheus
And the equinox of eternal time
You rise with the thrust and strength of Atlas
And challenge the solar sun with brightness
Like the Pyramids you are full of secrets
They stand in the desert sands
Ubiquitous as hands
Reaching for the stars
Remaining silent monumental monoliths
Bequeathed to the desert
From another time
Not built but born
Now beleaguered, bereft and benign

You are the one
Compelling in all counsel
A total Master Class with solitary distinction
A transgressor is in dire plight of extinction
You fill all voids with fervour and compunction
And fulfil all prophecies and functions
This strength of heart and mind

An inflection of some other kind
Assyrian in total techniques
And cloaked in compounding physiques
Instantly chilling mystique with ease
And with a look an opponent you freeze
The inexplicable still unexplained and unfathomed

The Buddha Guardian

I am the Guardian of the Buddha
The greatest of the greatest
Of all oratorios
Seek to know what He knows
Seek to see what He shows
Seek the walk that He goes
And listen with all the senses
When He talks the talk He knows
His wisdom is extensive
His lifetime is extended
His passion is expansive
His vision is exacting
Guard well all the knowledge
For the answers have been foraged
Throughout the Universe's Forest
Where the seeds have lain there dormant
For many weary years
For eyes that have been prying
Have ended up there crying
And ears that have been eavesdropping
Have been caught there on the hopping
So bear in mind the nature of the call
For if you fall it is a long way there to fall

Space Travellers

Don't let the sun go down on heartache
Let Venus brightly shine the night
A paternoster through the traumas
The flight path to the midnight light
A pathway strong and straight as arrows
As prophetic as the tarots
Luminous and illuminated
All of aeons as yet have waited
Holding breath that is abated
Permanent like Pharaohs fated
Star struck as in the words
That all ears have always heard
Like lightning trapped within a bottle
Power's centrifugal force doth topple
Taking secrets to the ground
Of the Snake King that is found
Murder of the first degree
From the vengeance they did flee
Swiftly there to a Pyramid Kingdom
Swiftly as a magic eye
Time was tagged and used as transport
A time machine from in the sky
Laden images did travel
Faster than the eye unravels

Pioneers from outer space
From their parallel life race
Journeyed here from space and time
On the radio wave energy line
Space to base in just an instant
Brought their colonising instinct
To the land of grains of sand
For there no one to see them land
Atmosphere accessed by light beams
Of the nuclear powered scout teams
Adapted unilaterally
Shed their cosmogeometry
Instinctive head for their survival
Enslaved immediate native idles
Night raiders built their epitaphic tombs
With cosmic plans of a hundred rooms
Slow breeding could not make the grade
In ethnic homes they were Solar made
They tried with Solar channelled light
But it did not help them in their plight
Their kingdom fell in disarray
For their sorrows again must pay
They brought with them their plans and worlds
As from their galaxy they were hurled
Their maxim would be to there return
But from here to there their crafts did burn
a-nuclear in physical matter
So all their energies did scatter
And mighty did lay upon the ground
The markings there that we have found

Cosmic Skin

Infinitesimal the Universe's fragments
Intangible upon the Cosmic skin
So undetectable the raging of the atoms
So unorthodox the power set within
But such a convoluted power
It explodes within the hour
But of madness –
No a sign of such a very human thing
For He – with all His power –
Is a luminescent Cosmogenic Crystal Ring
Highly explosive to the touch
Compelled to do so much
Aggressive, with a grudge
And suspicious of the sound of moving clouds
He's as loyal as own blood
And His strength would drown the mighty flood
And He would fight the raging fire
With just a blade
I do not have to think
We are sealed
With blood our link
My witness there – the Moon –
As out of leaden sky
At me she blinks

Age of Time

Through the passing age of time
There vibrates the call sublime
High frequency that travels fast
Impulse that for aeons lasts
Twined as ivy's climbing Ninja
Subtle as the air within you
Silently as sun arising
Drops the night just as surprising
Contrasts sharp as silver blade
Then gentle as the forest glade
Tempting you to wait and rest
And seats you like a trusted guest
Then violent tempest rends the air
And you are back there in the snare
And all its horror there it vents
So never rest your sole defence
The fire and flames leap ever higher
And touch you with the peril dire
Fortitude
Plenitude
Are your desire
I'll touch the sky
To make the Pie
Peacocks and butterflies
Personification of peaceful living

That to you is what I'll be giving
Languid grace
And graceful lives
Will be forthcoming
As bees to hives

Spirit of Freedom

And who is He
Who casts a watching eye
Endeavouring to see
And solve the aeons' mystery?
It is the holy spirit
The winged soul of the Cosmos
Whose spirit is freedom
Whose soul is courage
And whose life is eternal
Only mortalised for avengement
The Grand Buddha
The Master of achievement
The Ring of all Life
Monumental in strength
Immense in quality
The Physician of the Soul of the Cosmic Realm
All things in place
A place for all things

Sun, Moon and Stars

The sun has the Universe in which to sweep
Stars have the Night Sky in which to keep
Their eyes on the world in which we sleep
The moon has shadows in which to weep
But where do we find the treasure trove steps
That reach from earth to the heavenly depths?
The steps of brass
With edges of bronze
With silver and gold
In the great beyonds
The platinum lanterns show the way
With the diamond lights as bright as day
Just keep to the path
That the Angels show
It's clear and bright
And is white as snow
Do not let fright
Make you take flight
Just make your way
From night to day
Your senses recover
Equilibrium sets
And riches replace
The oldest of debts

Ladder to the Moon and Stars

The passage of the light
Doth pass through all the stars
Transverses all the planets
From Pluto back to Mars
With effort gargantuan
With childlike faith in strength
You put your trust in intuition
As you have your whole life length
Do not doubt in your ability
Do not waver in your intent
The passage of the light
Your messages have sent
The Crystal tree doth shimmer
With the gems you've placed upon
And there upon the top's the star
That all the rest it has outshone
It is written
And is spoken
It doth travel through the sky
That it is you whom I do rest upon
The pyramid of Pi

The Canopy of Wisdom

Give me guidance clear and coherent
Enlighten with wisdom the canopy that shelters
And let the opaque pearl transcend
And become a diamond of clarity so fine –
Put a diamond of genius in the soliloquy
And thread with gold my idealistic thoughts
Let the midnight sun reflect brilliance
And let the night sky be adorned
With brush strokes of a million stars
Let the light shine and dazzle
The eyes of the Black and Grisly Bear
Whose awesome presence pervades all
The Towers of Goodness balk at his aggression
Whilst the Towers of Hell manipulate his menacing demeanour
And channel his ferocious energy unto its dark and infernal well
Let the Power of Chi enter the Chinese circle
And with its entity of wisdom and articulate and ancient power
Deflect and de-energise the darkest of adversaries
The Chinese Snake and Dragon of Goodness
Can be used as the greatest amulets of the Universe
Call them up

They are the Guardians of the Cosmic Realm
And it is their antiquity among the Arts that creates their anathema
They shall look well after your needs
They are the Guardians of Bod
And shall serve you well

Desperately Seeking Triumph

I call to you desperately seeking triumph
Solace is scarcely skimming the surface of discord
Plantagenets abound but serve me not
My discordant soul is echoing throughout eons of time
This testing time is dragging me to the brink of the abyss
There is much that must be completed
My compass is failing me
I am disorientated to the extremes of all circumstances
The receptors must be decoding incorrectly
For there are no imprints that fit accordingly
Mercurial filaments are wildly disturbed
No permanent graph of the universal spectrum is coherently patterned
The geographical magnetic field must be malfunctioning in the vertical

The Universe's Hermaphrodite

Which of the Dimensions
Dost thou call upon to see?
I am the Universe's Hermaphrodite
Named Singularity
You can put all theories forward
You can move them up or down
You can move them side to side
Or turn them right around
But I am always there before you
And I can change things on a whim
Before your very eyes
Can change them back again
The string theory can tie you
All in knots behind your back
Because it's the 'Originalis' that you lack
There is a gap therein your knowledge
That can't be filled by what you know
And all that knowledge based on *If*
Covers up a deep dark well
You will have to go to my attorney
For He knows all the laws
From Abaris through to Newton's
He knows all the human flaws
He stands there in your midst

The answers there abound
For He can tell you how
To the questions you have found
But treat Him well and there respect Him
For I have sent Him there to tell
For however close you think the answers
Closer there are teeth of hell

Osiris Dawn

I will brush the sky with paint
And put a billion stars thereon
The Milky Way will glow
And I shall put the planets on
The moon and stars reflect the glory
Of the sun's amazing story
With the rising of Osiris every morn
There is a calendar that strikes the days
And pages flick past the moon's phase
As stars like diamonds sweet light
Do greet the night
There is a story
Of the glory
Of the dawning of the light
But it pales to mellow yellow
When it doth relate the fight
The Angel of the Night, 'tis told,
Was on his way to God
When Lucifer did hinder him
And did wrest from him the Pod
Within this Pod was everything
That Creation was about
But God had other problems
And did not hear His angel shout
Lucifer did sprinkle all Creation dust around
But did not theorise the relativity, and evil did abound

In horror and dismay
St Michael saved the day
And just in time he reached and caught
The antimatter compound salt
He split in just a second
The Heaven from the Earth
And sent Lucifer downward
Where to evil he gave birth
The Heaven there 'twas sent
On a spiral up in space
And ever more there's been
A good and evil place

The Grail

I am the Grail
Which men have always sought
I am the Grail
For which men have always fought
I am from time immemorial
Beyond the far beyond
And I am the possessor
Of your bond
I am from dreams impossible
And from the future that is past
And from that point in time
My memory is cast
It is all and doth encompass
The Quadrant Universe
So huge is my repository and my girth
I was not born or made
And in your understanding have no birth
Philosophers have wondered
From where their knowledge came
You may now look to me, for I take all the blame
I store immense emotions
And such knowledge, you would weep –
And to the intellectuals some vital wisdoms seep
But in my collective mind
All secrets sacred sacrosanct I keep

The Mighty Grail

I am the Mighty Grail
And in the Ultraverse I stand
Where everything is there
Within the reach of my right hand
In my bowl I hold
The copyright and verse
Of how and when created I
This Ultraverse
It consists of magnitudes
Of which you can only dream
And in my planning and matriculation
I have rounded out the scheme
Forthwith and there fourfolded
The Quadrant Angle Sits
All the while the asking of
Doth drive men from out their wits
I am manifolded
And also Omnipresent
For whilst I am of the Quadrant
I can never rest
And the heavier this burden
Doth Lay upon the Sea
The need and supplication
For succour calls to Me

I am much made
And have made much
And there the scale
Is multi such
I have a Guardian
Be there maid
Whence my sanctity by whom was saved
Mortal made
Or mortal mouse
Found sanctuary there within my House
Ever there and guarded well
The space between Heaven and Hell

Ultimate Grail

And of the Grail
Personification of power, light and deity
And the Angel of Death itself
Would be transfixed and captured
By the magnetism of the aura surrounding the insight
Which is the embodiment of the superordinate
Transposed
Translucent
Transcendental
And by the power of the Cross
Lifted high
And exalted to the heights of Jerusalem
Its namesake
And to the Most High
We do give utmost devotion and security
To see and to be accepted
Is the ultimate of appointments

Book of Changes

It is not a suppliant sinner
Whom now seeks
It is I the Shining Star
Who now doth speak
Look hard at all the pages
In the Sacred Book of Changes
And whose words upon the Golden Pages
Do you meet?

It is I the Golden Star
Whom straddled time
And travelled far
Built power forms
Created Storms and beat the Thorns

I've taken blades
Through time and space
The Universe I have replaced
And from my Stead I have been torn
Each time that I have been reborn

So now through Cosmic Law
I've reached and touched the floor
And lifted high the Earth
Fought and achieved for her rebirth

And now the Cosmic Law
Must deem to open Heaven's Door
Through all the trauma of the hour
Safe passage grant my Cosmic Power

These now are my commands
I have accomplished all demands
All is now redeemed
I have thwarted all Dark Forces' schemes.

Part Seven
Epilogue

Index

The Journey Home

You surround me in a sphere
A flowing life-pulse force
Its awesome magnitude expels
All other thoughts – as it compels
The heart and soul to journey forth
In complex expeditions
Spirit now no more fragmented
All thoughts now truly oriented:
One thought alone
To journey home
To where the lights of hidden force-fields comb
The Cosmos
Calling you back
To the origins of Birth and Creation;
To galaxies beyond the stars
Into the void
Where endless voyages are stirred
In aeons heartbeats only heard
The vastest exploratory steps unfurled
In mighty universal space
As yet unfathomed by the most exacting scholars
Of this embryonic race

Ark of the North

For your bravery and courage
There seems no just reward
For your patience and consistency
No edifice awarded
For your devotion to your goal
Your abilities of soul
Your total disregard of fearful ghouls
No medals handed out
No one your praises there to shout
No compromise of skills
No one to note each of your ills
You stand like mountain statue
With might and main and godly stature
And cast your glance of chance
At your domain
You can wither with a look
When quoting from the Book
And no one else durst stand within your rage
Your capabilities compelling
When from the White Book you are spelling
And Merlin and the Gods
Do stand and quake
You are as an atom in the making
And as a storm that's for the breaking
But your heart of gold too tender there to touch

It is there within a granite block for its protection
And for King of Hearts it has just won the election
It bleeds for needs of home
As through cosmic fields it roams
And just beats the beat of cosmic purity
Within it's dome
No Sea of Serenity yet can it sail on
No ark of the North yet is it's home
No coveted prize
No Pi in the skies
Just a workload that's high in its rise.

Glossary

Abaris	In Greek mythology the priest of Apollo, who fled Scythia for Greece to avoid a plague
Ambisonic	A means of recording whereby a single channel is encoded into four channels, all separately controllable
Angelo	Michelangelo Buonarroti (1475–1565). An Italian painter, sculptor, poet and architect
Armageddon	The final battle between good and evil fabled to occur at the end of he world
Atlas	In Greek mythology a Titan condemned to support the heavens on his shoulders by Zeus
Attila	(406–453) King of the Huns, who successfully invaded the Roman Empire
Bod/ Bodaham/ Bodahama	Ancient Indian monk, philosopher and sage; travelled overland to China and settled where He founded a teaching Monastery

	based on Wisdoms and Martial arts as a self-defence system to enable the monks to defend themselves with their farming weapons against the cruel and vicious War Lords of the regions. They protected the local communities and those too old or infirm to look after themselves
Book of Changes	(See *I Ching*)
Bridge of Sighs	A bridge over the Rio di Palazzo, in Venice, connecting the prison to the inquisitor's rooms within the palace; it's name, popularised by Lord Byron in the seventeenth century, supposedly deriving from the sighs of prisoners seeing freedom for the last time as they crossed to their cells
Chi	In Taoism the vital force that exists in all things
Cosmogenic	Produced by cosmic rays
Damocles	In Greek mythology a courtier to Dionysus who was forced to sit beneath a sword held by a single hair in order to demonstrate the precarious nature of the king's position

David	(d. 962 b.c.)The second king of Israel who slew the giant Goliath to succeed *Saul*
Deuteronomy	The fifth book of the Old Testament containing the second statement of the law laid down by Moses
Dionysus	In Greek mythology the god of wine
Elijah	A Hebrew prophet
Eros	Greek god of love; son of Aphrodite
Gethsemane	In the New Testament the garden near Jerusalem where Jesus was betrayed
Hades	In Greek mythology the god of the underworld; hell itself
Hebe	In Greek mythology the goddess of youth and spring
Heptateuch	The first seven books of the Old Testament
Heracles	Also Hercules; in Greek mythology the son of Zeus and Alcmene who performed twelve legendary labours for the Argive king Eurytheus

Huguenot	A French protestant during the religious wars of the sixteenth and seventeenth centuries
I Ching	Ancient Chinese book of interrelated hexagrams and commentaries used for divination and embodying Taoist philosophy by describing all actions in terms of yin and yang. Also called The Book of Changes
Jason	In Greek mythology an heroic figure who led the Argonauts to steal the Golden Fleece from the king of Colchis
Juno	Roman goddess of woman and the moon; married to Jupiter
Jupiter	Fifth planet from the sun; Roman god of agriculture
Kublai Khan	The first Mongol emperor who founded that dynasty (1215–1294)
Luxor	A city in central Egypt on the Nile; site of the Luxor Temple
Magna Carta	The charter of civil rights granted by King John in 1215
Magnetronic	Of a microwave tube, where electrons gather and via their reactions to magnetic and electric fields produce heat

Mars	Fourth planet from the sun; Roman god of war
Medicis	Italian noble family, which produced three popes and two queens of France
Merlin	The magician who acted as advisor to King Arthur
Midas	The fabled king of Phrygia to whom Dionysus gave the power to turn everything hr touched to gold
Morpheus	The god of dreams in Ovid's *Metamorphoses*
Orpheus	In Greek mythology a poet and musician whose music could move inanimate things and who almost managed to rescue his wife, Eurydice, from Hades
Osiris	Egyptian god of the underworld, who annually died and was resurrected
Pandora's Box	In Greek mythology a box that Zeus gave to Pandora and forbade her to open. When her curiosity overcame her and she opened the box, she released all mankind's misery

Pitimus	A part of the power of the Dark Force
Plantagenets	A line of English kings, from Henry II (1154) to Richard III (1485)
Pluto	The ninth planet from the sun; Roman god of the underworld
Saturn	Sixth planet from the sun; Roman god supreme
Scarlet Pimpernel	Hero of the novel of the same name by Baroness Emma Orczy. The Scarlet Pimpernel (a.k.a. Sir Percival Blackeney) rescued countless victims during the 'Reign of Terror' stage of the French Revolution from Madame Guillotine
Scorpius	Also Scorpio; a zodiacal constellation
Simoom	A dry, hot, sand-laden wind of the Sahara and Arabian deserts
Sirius	The brightest star in the sky, also called the Dog Star
Solomon	A king of Israel in the tenth century B.C. famed for his wisdom

T'ai Chi — Chinese Martial Art form

Templars — The Knights Templar; in 1119 nine French knights took monastic oaths to protect pilgrims to the holy places; so called because their base in Jerusalem stood on the site of the old Temple of Solomon

Thor — The Norse god of thunder

Thoth — The Egyptian god of the moon and of wisdom, depicted with the head of an ibis

Titan — In Greek mythology, a member of a clan of giants who ruled the heavens before being overthrown by Zeus

Tsars — Emperors of Russia prior to the revolution of 1917

Valhalla — In Scandinavian mythology, where those favoured by the gods (usually heroes) go when they die

Venus — Second planet from the sun; Roman goddess of beauty and love

Xanadu — A mythical place in Samuel Taylor Coleridge's poem *Kublai Khan*

Yin Yang	In Chinese dualist philosophy, Yin is the passive feminine element and Yang the active male element

Index of First Lines

Printed in the United Kingdom
by Lightning Source UK Ltd.
117057UKS00001B/46-93